The Big Book Of Atlanta Braves Trivia

By Monica Hamlet

TM

We hope you enjoy your purchase. Please feel welcome to give us your feedback as we would be able to come up with more creative content!

INTRODUCTION

The Atlanta Braves is an American professional baseball team based in the Atlanta metropolitan area. The Braves compete in Major League Baseball (MLB) as a member club of the National League (NL) East division. Since 2017, their home stadium has been Truist Park (formerly SunTrust Park), located 10 miles (16 km) northwest of downtown Atlanta in Cobb County, Georgia. The Braves play spring training games at CoolToday Park in North Port, Florida.

The name "Braves" originates from a term for a Native American warrior. They are nicknamed "the Bravos", and often referred to as "America's Team" in reference to the team's games being broadcast on the nationally available TBS from the 1970s until 2007, giving the team a nationwide fan base.

If you are a big fan of the Atlanta Braves, it's time to check out ***The Big Book of Atlanta Braves Trivia*** with all the interesting quizzes and facts you might not know!

Table of Contents

Quiz Time!

1. Who was the first player in the franchise's history that was inducted into the Hall of Fame after playing for the Braves, but not necessarily inducted as a Brave?
   A. Ted Williams
   B. Babe Ruth
   C. Hank Aaron
   D. Jose Canseco

2. Who was the first Braves pitcher to win 350 games in their uniform?
   A. Gaylord Perry
   B. Warren Spahn
   C. Stan Musial
   D. Tom Seaver

3. In which year did the franchise move from Boston to Milwaukee?
   A. 1994
   B. 1915
   C. 1892
   D. 1953

4. The Braves' franchise was not always called the Braves. The team was one of eight inaugural members of the new National League in 1876. What was the name of the team?
   A. Gloves
   B. Indians
   C. Red Caps
   D. Green Stockings

5. In which season did the franchise win its first World Series title?
   A. 1886
   B. 1985
   C. 1951
   D. 1914

6. Wearing a Braves uniform, who was the first player to hit 50 home runs in a season?
   A. Andruw Jones
   B. Willie Mays
   C. Hank Aaron
   D. Harmon Killebrew

7. The great Hank Aaron set more than a few franchise records. One that he did not set was the first Braves player to strike out 1500 times in their team's uniform. Who set this distinction?
   A. Joe Adcock
   B. Dale Murphy
   C. Rod Carew
   D. Tony Oliva

8. Who was the franchise's first manager to win 2000 career games with the team?
   A. Tom Lasorda
   B. Joe Torre
   C. Billy Martin
   D. Bobby Cox

9. After moving the franchise to Atlanta in 1966, which year did the team give their Atlanta fans their first World Series crown?
   A. 1995
   B. 1986
   C. 1967
   D. 2008

10. Who was the franchise's first player to win the National League MVP Award?
    A. Johnny Evers
    B. Wade Boggs
    C. Bill Buckner
    D. George Brett

11. The Braves franchise joined the National League with the league's inception in 1876, but this wasn't the first time that the world saw this franchise. Did they begin it all in 1871 under the name of the Boston Red Stockings in which league?
    A. National Association
    B. Federal League
    C. American Federation
    D. Federation of National Players

12. After the franchise joined the National League in 1876 as the Boston Red Caps to continue their winning ways, they won two NL pennants, then changed their name in 1883 to what name?
    A. Boston Gophers
    B. Boston Beaneaters
    C. Boston Blue Jays
    D. Boston Tea Parties

13. What Brave had "Smooth" by Santana as his intro music?
    A. Gary Sheffield
    B. Marcus Giles
    C. Andruw Jones
    D. Vinny Castilla

14. Which of the following never managed the Braves?
    A. Frank Selee
    B. Casey Stengel
    C. Sparky Anderson
    D. Bill McKechnie

15. Which of the following pitchers retired with the most wins for the Braves?
    A. Phil Niekro
    B. Warren Spahn
    C. Tom Glavine
    D. Whitey Ford

16. Throughout the Braves' history, they would appear as the NL winners only in spurts, then in 1991, this manager would begin a streak of 14 division titles in 15 seasons. Who was this manager?
    A. Joe Torre
    B. Lum Harris
    C. Chuck Tanner
    D. Bobby Cox

17. The great name of Hank Aaron is truly associated with the Braves. He hit 733 career home runs in a Braves uniform, and 755 overall. How many times did his greatness hit 50 home runs in a season?
    A. He never did
    B. 9
    C. 3
    D. 6

18. After 13 seasons in Milwaukee, the club moved to and played in Atlanta in which year?
    A. 1982
    B. 2001
    C. 1943
    D. 1966

19. Only one player in the Braves' history played for the team in Boston, Milwaukee, and Atlanta. Who was this third baseman?
    A. Eddie Mathews
    B. Felipe Alou
    C. Bob Horner
    D. Chipper Jones

20. The 2007 Braves finished third in the NL East. Which 40-year old veteran went 14-8 for the team?
    A. JASON Isringhausen
    B. John Smoltz
    C. Troy Percival
    D. Ramon Ortiz

21. In the scorebook, position 1 is the pitcher. This big right-hander won more games in Milwaukee than any Brave other than Hall of Famer Warren Spahn. He was the MVP of the 1957 World Series and claimed three of the Champions' four wins. Who was he?
    A. Johnny Sain
    B. Lew Burdette
    C. Kid Nichols
    D. Joey Jay

22. Catcher -- A favorite backstop in Milwaukee was an eleven-time All-Star who held the position for almost the entire Braves' stay in Brew City. Who was he?
    A. Ed Bailey
    B. Frank Torre
    C. Del Crandall
    D. Sherm Lollar

23. Which Braves starting pitcher had "Crawling in the Dark", by Hoobastank, as his intro music?
    A. Greg Maddux
    B. Horacio Ramirez
    C. Shane Reynolds
    D. Russ Ortiz

24. Second base – He is a real utility player whose 11-year career included 326 games at second, 180 games at shortstop, 143 at third, and 156 in the outfield. In 1953, he roomed with Henry Aaron on the Jacksonville Braves before becoming teammates in Milwaukee. Who was he?
    A. Felix Mantilla
    B. Tommy Aaron
    C. Nellie Fox
    D. Del Rice

25. Third base -- Hall of Famer Ed Mathews dominated that position for the Braves in Milwaukee. But there is the one who is first joined the team in 1961, and in the Braves' last season in Milwaukee in '65 he won 24 games, the most single-season wins by any Braves hurler in the franchise's stay in Cream City. This Brave became the only pitcher to hit two grand slams in one game in the 20th Century. Who is he?

A. Tony Cloninger
B. Bob Buhl
C. Don McMahon
D. Gene Conley

26. In 1955, he led the NL in doubles and in the '57 Series he and Aaron led the Braves in runs scored with 5 each. Who was this son of a Russian immigrant?
   A. Carl Sawatski
   B. Johnny Logan
   C. Carl Yastrzemski
   D. Bill Mazeroski

27. This outfield Milwaukee Brave face was a swift center fielder who led the NL in stolen bases three consecutive years, in triples twice and in runs scored once. Who was this Alabama native who led off a game with a home run twelve times?
   A. Wally Moon
   B. Dave Jolly
   C. Bill Bruton
   D. Biff Pocoroba

28. In August of 1957, a rookie came up with the Braves and batted .556 in his first twelve games and totaled 5 home runs and 19 RBI. Who was this South Carolina native who batted .403 in 41 games and earned the nickname "Hurricane" based on his play and the storm that struck his home state in 1954?

    A. Bob Hazle
    B. Harry Hanebrink
    C. Randy Hundley
    D. Fred Haney

29. This outfielder played in Milwaukee for the first five full seasons of an 11-year career. Who was this Braves outfielder who batted .330 in 1958 with 24 home runs and 74 RBI?

    A. Ernie Johnson
    B. Harvey Kuenn
    C. Wes Covington
    D. Al Kaline

30. This Brave broke into Major League Baseball as a catcher in 1962 as a Milwaukee Brave. You may know him best by his voice, like his quote as Harry Doyle: "Juuuust a bit outside." Which of these four golden-throated ones finishes our quiz?
    A. Harry Caray
    B. Dizzy Dean
    C. Tim McCarver
    D. Bob Uecker

31. The franchise began in the National Association in 1871 as the Boston Red Stockings. From there it was on to the new National League in 1876. Finally, the franchise moved to which city in 1953, and played there until the mid-1960s?
    A. St. Louis
    B. Ft Wayne
    C. Portland
    D. Milwaukee

32. The franchise moved to Atlanta in 1966, making it the franchise's third city that they would root down in. Who was the only player of the franchise to play in all three cities with the team?
    A. Warren Spahn
    B. Eddie Mathews
    C. Duke Snider
    D. Harmon Killebrew

33. Pitcher Tony Cloninger proved that he had an arm in 1965 by going 24-11 in Milwaukee. The new air in 1966 must have done something for him. What did he do to make it into the record books in the season?
    A. He hit two grand slams in one game
    B. Cloninger was ejected a record eight times in the season
    C. Tony threw nine shutouts in the season
    D. He threw 55-1/3 consecutive scoreless innings

34. Although the 1969 season would belong to the New York Mets, the Braves won their NL Western Division. They had only one 20-game winner in the season. Who was it?
    A. Lindy McDaniel
    B. Bob Friend
    C. Sal Maglie
    D. Phil Niekro

35. After over 100 into the 1972 season, manager Lum Harris was fired. Which former Braves players would take over the team, and manage them in three seasons?
    A. Johnny Logan
    B. Lew Burdette
    C. Eddie Mathews
    D. Warren Spahn

36. 1975 was a shock to Braves fans. This would be the first season without the great Hank Aaron, who was traded to the Milwaukee Brewers. The team had no starter hit .300 in the season. The 1976 season wasn't too promising either, as the Braves finished last in the National League West. They had only one starter hit over .300. Who was it?
    A. Willie Montanez
    B. Bob Aspromonte
    C. Orlando Cepeda
    D. Clete Boyer

37. 1977 was the worst season that the franchise experienced in over 30 years, going 61-101. With no starter coming close to .300, the Braves had only one pitcher win in double-figures during the season. Who was it?
    A. Phil Niekro
    B. Pascual Perez
    C. Bob Walk
    D. Steve Bedrosian

38. Who would take over the helm of the Braves in 1978, in his first managerial job, and later change the history of the ballclub?
    A. Herman Franks
    B. Joe Torre
    C. Bobby Cox
    D. Ken Boyer

39. The Braves had a 20-year old rookie third baseman start the season for them in 1978. He would go on to win the NL Rookie of the Year award. Who was it?
    A. Bob Horner
    B. Cito Gaston
    C. Darrel Chaney
    D. Jimmy Wynn

40. The Braves had only two winning seasons in the 1970s, and 1979 would not be one of them. Although finishing last with a 66-94 record, they still had a 20-game winner, five players hit home runs in double-figures, and which outfielder led the team with 192 hits?
    A. Gary Mathews
    B. Dusty Baker
    C. Darrell Evans
    D. Davey Johnson

41. On April 22nd, 1876, the Boston franchise participated in the very first game in National League history when they visited which team?
    A. New York Mutuals
    B. St Louis Brown Stockings
    C. Hartford Dark Blues
    D. Philadelphia Athletics

42. Who was the first manager in the franchise's history, who led them to pennants in 1877 and 1878?
    A. John Morrill
    B. Harry Wright
    C. Frank Selee
    D. Fred Tenney

43. After a number of years in the National League cellar, the "Miracle Braves" shocked the baseball world by winning the 1914 World Series. Who were their opponents in the Fall Classic?
    A. Boston Red Sox
    B. Detroit Tigers
    C. New York Yankees
    D. Philadelphia Athletics

44. Which legendary New York Yankees player ended his career with the Boston Braves in 1935?
    A. Lou Gehrig
    B. Carl Mays
    C. Lefty Gomez
    D. Babe Ruth

45. Where did the Braves play their home games between 1915 and 1952?
    A. Huntington Avenue Grounds
    B. Fenway Park
    C. Braves Field
    D. South End Grounds

46. The Braves won their first NL pennant in1914. In 1948, unlike their first World Series appearance, this one ended in defeat to which team?
    A. Cleveland Indians
    B. Washington Senators
    C. New York Yankees
    D. Boston Red Sox

47. Who hit the most home runs in the franchise's history?
    A. Fred Tenney
    B. Tommy Holmes
    C. Wally Berger
    D. Sam Jethroe

48. Which pitcher won the most games in the franchise's history?
    A. Kid Nichols
    B. Vic Willis
    C. Warren Spahn
    D. Dick Rudolph

49. Excluding doubleheaders, the largest crowd for a Braves home game turned up for a 1948 game against which team?
    A. Philadelphia Phillies
    B. New York Giants
    C. Chicago Cubs
    D. Brooklyn Dodgers

50. Which Braves starting pitcher had "Crawling in the Dark", by Hoobastank, as his intro music?
    A. Greg Maddux
    B. Horacio Ramirez
    C. Shane Reynolds
    D. Russ Ortiz

51. Which Atlanta Braves pitcher made his MLB debut on July 14, 1997, and amassed a total of 2,083 career strikeouts in his career?
    A. John Smoltz
    B. Tom Glavine
    C. Kevin Milwood
    D. Tim Hudson

52. John Smoltz had an illustrious career as a pitcher for the Atlanta Braves. Which team originally drafted John Smoltz during the 1985 amateur draft?
    A. Montreal Expos
    B. Boston Red Sox
    C. Detroit Tigers
    D. Atlanta Braves

53. Which Atlanta Braves manager earned four Manager of the Year awards and led the Atlanta Braves to a win in the 1995 World Series?
    A. Bobby Cox
    B. Bobby Valentine
    C. Joe Torre
    D. Fredi González

54. Which Braves pitcher, who wore the number 31, won four consecutive National League Cy Young awards?
    A. Greg Maddux
    B. Kevin Milwood
    C. John Smoltz
    D. Tom Glavine

55. What was the name of the original mascot of the Milwaukee and Atlanta Braves from the 1950s until 1986?
    A. Rally
    B. Bobby the Brave
    C. Tommy Hawk
    D. Chief Noc-A-Homa

56. This 1999 National League MVP played 19 seasons in Atlanta. What was the name of the Braves' third baseman who retired at the end of the 2012 season?
    A. Coco Crisp
    B. Chipper Jones
    C. Lyle Overbay
    D. Dan Uggla

57. Ryan Klesko played for the Atlanta Braves from 1992-1999 and was a member of the 1995 World Series team. What primary infield position did Klesko play throughout the majority of his career?
    A. Shortstop
    B. Third Baseman
    C. First Baseman
    D. Pitcher

58. Which baseball legend played for the Atlanta Braves and got death threats when he got close to breaking a record?
    A. Tom Seaver
    B. Mickey Lolich
    C. Phil Niekro
    D. Hank Aaron

59. In 1994, the Atlanta Braves retired the #3 jersey worn by a 15-year member of the Braves franchise. What was the name of the seven-time All-Star, who wore the Braves #3?
    A. Jackie Robinson
    B. Tom Glavine
    C. Dale Murphy
    D. Hank Aaron

60. Andrés Galarraga ended his Major League career with 399 home runs. Which famous Detroit Tigers right fielder ended his career with the same number of home runs as Galarraga?
    A. Hank Greenberg
    B. Mickey Lolich
    C. Al Kaline
    D. Sparky Anderson

61. Which city did the Braves call home before relocating to Milwaukee for the 1953 season?
    A. Baltimore
    B. Brooklyn
    C. Boston
    D. Philadelphia

62. The Braves' first game in Milwaukee took place on April 14th, 1953, versus which team?
    A. St Louis Cardinals
    B. Cincinnati Reds
    C. New York Giants
    D. Pittsburgh Pirates

63. Which stadium did the Braves call home during their tenure in Milwaukee?
    A. Miller Park
    B. Lloyd Street Park
    C. Braves Field
    D. County Stadium

64. Who took over as manager from Charlie Grimm 46 games into the 1956 season, and led them to World Series glory the following year?
    A. Bobby Bragan
    B. Tommy Holmes
    C. Fred Haney
    D. Chuck Dressen

65. The Braves won their first World Series for 43 years in 1957. Who were their series opponents?
    A. Boston Red Sox
    B. New York Yankees
    C. Baltimore Orioles
    D. Detroit Tigers

66. Who was the MVP of the 1957 World Series?
    A. Eddie Matthews
    B. Frank Torre
    C. Hank Aaron
    D. Lew Burdette

67. What Brave had "Ta'haciendio Frio" by Pochy y Su Coco Band Familia, as his intro music?
    A. Rafael Furcal
    B. Andruw Jones
    C. Vinny Castilla
    D. Javy Lopez

68. Which pitcher won the most games for the Milwaukee Braves?
    A. Don McMahon
    B. Lew Burdette
    C. Warren Spahn
    D. Tony Cloninger

69. The largest crowd for a Braves home game in Milwaukee was 48,642 versus which team?
    A. Chicago Cubs
    B. San Francisco Giants
    C. Philadelphia Phillies
    D. Los Angeles Dodgers

70. Amazingly, despite never having a losing season in Milwaukee, crowd numbers slumped in the early 1960s. In 1965, the owners announced that they would be relocating the team in time for the 1966 season. Which southern city was to be their new home?
    A. Atlanta
    B. New Orleans
    C. Miami
    D. Memphis

71. In what three cities did the Braves win the 1914, 1957, and 1995 World Series?
    A. Boston, Milwaukee, and Atlanta
    B. Canton, Kansas City, and Atlanta
    C. New York, Baltimore, and Miami
    D. Sioux City, St. Louis, and Atlanta

72. In the last place on July 4, 1914, the Boston Braves steamrolled the National League for the rest of the season, taking the National League title by 10 games over the New York Giants. They then went on to win the World Championship in the first complete World Series sweep in major-league baseball. What nickname, also applied to another National League team 55 years later, did the 1914 Braves become known by?
    A. the Go-Go Braves
    B. the Miracle Braves
    C. the Big Redskin Machine
    D. the Back Bay Bombers

73. Who were two Hall of Famers on the 1914 Braves team (although one of them was better known as a Chicago Cub)?
    A. Babe Ruth and Lou Gehrig
    B. Hack Wilson and Kid Nichols
    C. Lloyd and Paul Waner
    D. Johnny Evers and Rabbit Maranville

74. What Brave had "In Da Club" by 50 Cent as his intro music?
    A. Gary Sheffield
    B. Rafael Furcal
    C. Vinny Castilla
    D. Marcus Giles

75. Whom did the Braves beat in the 1957 World Series?
    A. Kansas City Royals
    B. Chicago White Sox
    C. New York Yankees
    D. Baltimore Orioles

76. What Brave had "Forever" by Kid Rock as his intro music?
    A. Marcus Giles
    B. Andruw Jones
    C. Chipper Jones
    D. Gary Sheffield

77. Which Hall of Fame infielder, traded from the Giants to the Braves in 1957, may have been the key ingredient that propelled Milwaukee to world series appearances in 1957 and 1958? Most associated with the Cardinals, he was part of five World Series winners, all of which won their championships in seven games.
    A. Bob "Hurricane" Hazle
    B. Eddie Mathews
    C. Bobby Thomson
    D. Red Schoendienst

78. The Braves moved from Milwaukee to Atlanta in 1966. The Braves won Western Division titles in 1969 and 1982 but did not make it to the World Series in

either year. Beginning in 1991, Atlanta won 14 consecutive division titles, the first three in the Western Division and the last 11 in the Eastern Division. What team kept the Braves out of the playoffs in 1994?

    A.   There were no playoffs.
    B.   Los Angeles Dodgers
    C.   Montreal Expos
    D.   Philadelphia Phillies

79. What team, which led the American League in batting average, runs scored, home runs, and stolen bases, did the Braves beat in six games to win the 1995 World Series?

    A.   New York Yankees
    B.   Boston Red Sox
    C.   Oakland Athletics
    D.   Cleveland Indians

80. On January 8, 2014, what two members of the 1995 Braves World Champions were voted into Baseball's Hall of Fame, in their first year of eligibility?

    A.   Fred McGriff and Terry Pendleton
    B.   Chipper Jones and John Smoltz
    C.   Greg Maddux and Tom Glavine
    D.   David Justice and Dale Murphy

81. Atlanta Stadium opened for business on April 9, 1965, with the Milwaukee Braves playing a 3-game exhibition series against which American League team?
    A. Baltimore Orioles
    B. New York Yankees
    C. Detroit Tigers
    D. Boston Red Sox

82. For much of the 1980s, there was a person dressed in a monk's outfit who led Braves cheers atop the dugout roof. He was named Brother who?
    A. Steven
    B. Phillip
    C. David
    D. Francis

83. Who tossed out the ceremonial first pitch in the Braves' first Atlanta game on April 12, 1966?
    A. Atlanta Mayor Ivan Allen, Jr.
    B. James Brown
    C. Dr. Martin Luther King, Jr.
    D. GA State Senator Jimmy Carter

84. Who hit the first upper deck home run in Atlanta Stadium?
    A. Willie Smith
    B. Hank Aaron
    C. Willie Stargell
    D. Wes Parker

85. The final out of Phil Niekro's August 5, 1973, no-hitter vs. the Padres was made by who?
    A. Dave Roberts
    B. Dave Winfield
    C. Nate Colbert
    D. Cito Gaston

86. In the early 1980s, Chief Noc-a-Homa had a female assistant mascot with him. Her name was Princess Win-a-Lotta.
    A. True
    B. False

87. Who was on deck when Hank Aaron hit home run #715 on April 8, 1974?
    A. Ralph Garr
    B. Paul Casanova
    C. Dusty Baker
    D. Davey Johnson

88. For the 1990 season, which Southern celebrity was doing TV, newspaper, and radio ads for the Braves?
    A. Jeff Foxworthy
    B. John Schneider (aka Bo Duke)
    C. Roy Clark
    D. Jim Varney (aka Ernest P. Worrell)

89. Which was determined to be the official cause of Atlanta Stadium's pre-game fire at the club level, on July 20, 1993?
    A. A cigarette dropped on the carpet
    B. A spilled Sterno can
    C. Electrical short
    D. Arson

90. Which Brave caught the final out of the 1995 World Series, to give Atlanta their first World Series title?
    A. Dave Justice
    B. Marquis Grissom
    C. Chipper Jones
    D. Dwight Smith

91. What Brave had "Move" by Ludacris featuring Mystikal as his intro music?
    A. Javy Lopez
    B. Robert Fick
    C. Chipper Jones
    D. Andruw Jones

92. What Brave had "Family Affair" by Mary J. Blige as his intro music?
    A. Vinny Castilla
    B. Robert Fick
    C. Javy Lopez
    D. Rafael Furcal

93. In the 1996 Fall Classic, Andruw Jones became the first player to do what?
    A. Hit for the cycle in a World Series game
    B. Hit an infield home run
    C. Homer in his 1st 2 career World Series at-bats
    D. Play all 9 positions in a World Series game

94. Dave Justice is remembered for hitting the series' winning home run in game 6 of the 1995 World Series against Cleveland. Who did he hit it off?
    A. Orel Hershiser
    B. Jim Poole
    C. Dennis Martinez
    D. Alan Embree

95. Who pitched a 10-inning complete game to earn the Twins the game 7 wins?
    A. John Smoltz
    B. Jack Morris
    C. Kevin Tapani
    D. Julio Santana

96. How many games were decided by 1 run in the 1991 World Series?
    A. 7
    B. 5
    C. 3
    D. 1

97. Who was the Braves' opponent in the 1958 World Series?
    A. Cleveland Indians
    B. Boston Red Sox
    C. New York Yankees
    D. Baltimore Orioles

98. In what stadium did the Braves clinch their first World Series title?
    A. Braves Field
    B. Fenway Park
    C. Shibe Park
    D. South Ends Ground

99. Who led the Braves in home runs during the 1995 World Series?
    A. Ryan Klesko
    B. Dave Justice
    C. Fred McGriff
    D. Chipper Jones

100. How many National League pennants did the Braves win in the 1990s?
    - A. 8
    - B. 3
    - C. 5
    - D. 6

101. What Brave had "Here I Go" by Mystikal, as his intro music?
    - A. Marcus Giles
    - B. Chipper Jones
    - C. Gary Sheffield
    - D. Robert Fick

102. What Braves relief (or closing pitcher) had "Thunderstruck" by AC/DC as his intro music?
    - A. John Smoltz
    - B. Trey Hodges
    - C. Ray King
    - D. Kevin Gryboski

103. One player in Brave history played for the Boston, Milwaukee, and the Atlanta Braves. Who was he?
    - A. Warren Spahn
    - B. Lew Burdette
    - C. Hank Aaron
    - D. Eddie Mathews

104. The Milwaukee Braves broke many attendance records in their short Milwaukee stay. How many seasons did the Braves attract 2 million people?
    A. 3
    B. 4
    C. 5
    D. 1

105. Where in Florida did the Milwaukee Braves have their spring training facilities located?
    A. Jacksonville
    B. Palm Springs
    C. Bradenton
    D. Huntington Beach

106. Behind the centerfield fence at County Stadium, the Braves home, there were a group of trees. What was it called?
    A. Milwaukee's Woods
    B. Braves' Forest
    C. Perini's Woods
    D. Aaron's Amazon

107. When the All-Star game was played in Milwaukee in 1955, which team won the game, and who hit the walk-off home run?
    A. NL; Stan Musial
    B. NL; Ernie Banks
    C. NL; Hank Aaron
    D. AL; Mickey Mantle

108. Which short term Braves player later became a play-by-play announcer for the Milwaukee Brewers?
    A. Hank Aaron
    B. Bob Uecker
    C. Frank Torre
    D. Felix Mantilla

109. Hank Aaron and Eddie Mathews were two hard-hitting teammates. Hank ended with 755 home runs, but how many did Matthews hit?
    A. 475
    B. 565
    C. 600
    D. 512

110. Who did the Braves play in their final game in Milwaukee?
    A. Chicago Cubs
    B. Los Angeles Dodgers
    C. Philadelphia Phillies
    D. Pittsburgh Pirate

111. What two positions did Chipper Jones regularly play for the Braves?
    A. Shortstop and center field
    B. Shortstop and catcher
    C. Third and right field
    D. Third base and left field

112. What team did the Braves acquire Gary Sheffield from?
    A. Florida Marlins
    B. San Diego Padres
    C. Chicago Cubs
    D. Los Angeles Dodgers

113. Chipper and Andruw Jones are related?
    A. True
    B. False

114. Which 2001 pitcher was known for his running out of the bullpen to the mound?
    A. Greg Maddux
    B. John Smoltz
    C. John Rocker
    D. Tom Glavine

115. What position did Andres Galarraga play during the 2000 season with the Braves?
    A. Second base
    B. Third base
    C. Right field
    D. First base

116. What was the name of the ballpark that the Braves moved to in 1997?
    A. Turner Field
    B. Metropolitan Stadium
    C. Enron Field
    D. Braves Stadium

117. How many feet is it to the left-field fence in their ballpark?
    A. 360
    B. 400
    C. 300
    D. 335

118. Do the Braves use a DH for every regular-season game?
    A. True
    B. False

119. What division of the National League did the Braves play in during the 2001 season?

    A. north

    B. west

    C. south

    D. east

120. 'Chipper' is Chipper Jones' real first name?

    A. True

    B. False

I. ATLANTA BRAVES FACTS

1. The Braves were one of eight founding teams in the National League when it began its franchise in 1876 as the Boston Red Caps. From there, the team would be bought and sold several times, undergo new nicknames such as the Beaneaters, Doves, Rustlers, Braves, Bees, and then finally back to the Braves.

2. 1914 is perhaps one of the best comeback stories in baseball lore. Dubbed the "Miracle Braves", the team found itself in last place on July 6th with a 27-40 record. The big comeback began as the Braves tore off an impressive 68-19 mark in their last 87 games, 10.5

games better than the New York Giants as they leap-frogged the teams ahead of them.

3. In that year of the miracle, the Boston Braves stormed into the World Series and swept the heavily favored Philadelphia A's in stunning fashion, 4-0. Afterward, Connie Mack disassembled the A's, culling the older players, some of which jumped ship anyways to greener pastures. The Braves would not reach the World Series for the next 34 seasons.

4. The Braves had returned to being just standard within the division for the next 30 plus years, eventually returning to respectability with manager Billy Southworth, who had gained fame by steering the great St. Louis Cardinal teams of the 1940s.

5. The National League Pennant was captured by the Braves in 1948, due mostly to the pitching of Warren Spahn and Johnny Sain. The often-heard mantra with Braves fans and the newspapers were, (Spahn and Sain and pray for rain). Which indicated the Braves were no good unless those two pitchers were on the mound.

6. In 1948, The Boston Braves locked up with the Cleveland Indians and lost in their second World Series to the tribe in 6 games.

7. For the next four years, the Braves began to lose more money, more fans and prompted owner Lou Perini to look around the country for a new place to move the Braves. Milwaukee seemed to be a good fit, away from the Red Sox.

8. The move of the Braves to Milwaukee was the first shift of a major league franchise since 1903 and it closed the book on an 81-year history the team had cemented in Boston. In the final game as the Boston Braves, the Braves ended in a 5-5 tie with the Brooklyn Dodgers at Ebbets Field on Sept. 28th, 1952. They left Boston with 10 Pennants and 1 World Series Championship.

9. The Braves came to Milwaukee and gave the city that was hungry for baseball another baseball team to root for. Free of any other baseball teams in the city taking fans and money away from the franchise as the Red Sox had in Boston, the Braves settled in County Stadium to begin what was thought to be a life-long relationship with the fans and city.

10. While there, the Braves had developed into a National League powerhouse in the 1950s with breakout stars such as Henry Aaron, Eddie Mathews leading the charge with a supporting cast of Joe Adcock and Del Crandall. The pitching staff had Braves vet Warren Spahn, Lew Burdette, and Bob Buhl. Aaron and Spahn

would capture MVP and Cy Young in 1957 respectively.

11. In the first game at County Stadium, the Braves shut out the Reds 2-0 on April 13th, 1953 on Max Surkont's 3-hit shutout. From there the Braves would play before 1,826,397 fans in that inaugural season in Milwaukee which, by the way, had set the National League attendance record for that time.

12. The team rolled in the 1950s winning back-to-back National League Pennants in 1957 and again in 1958. Both trips to the World Series saw the Braves and Yankees take the series to seven games. The Braves, led by Lew Burdette's 3 complete games in the World Series in 1957 captured the Braves' second World Series title. The team and the city of Milwaukee were overjoyed.

13. However, in 1958, the Braves and Yankees met once again the following year. Another World Series that would go the distance to the seventh game as the Braves failed to repeat as champs.

14. Just like in Boston, the fans began to slow at the gates and didn't fill the seats to watch the team that they loved and cheered during the 50's play. Attendance began to fall sharply and the new management decided that they would uproot the Braves and move

once again, maybe to a place that appreciated them more.

15. Wooed by the city of Atlanta, the Braves' front office decided that the south would be their new home. City officials were trying to lure major league teams down to Atlanta for some time and saw that the Braves were interested in leaving Milwaukee. One selling point was that the Braves would have no other baseball teams around and the radio and television markets were theirs.

16. The Braves announced that they were leaving the city of Milwaukee which made fans cry, spit and shout words of venom towards the management for the deed. But it was a business move for the team. Atlanta wanted to be the "Gateway to the South" and wanted the Braves as their centerpiece. A major league team would give the city a major league feel and make tourists look at the city as if they were growing up.

17. Having to wait out their lease in 1965, the Braves finally moved from Milwaukee after the lawsuits, the injunctions, and the public outcries to keep them there in Milwaukee. The Braves only drew just a little over half a million fans that year, although most of the fans did not go to the games out of protest. The poor attendance only made the case for the Braves'

ownership that the move to Atlanta was in the team's best interest.

18. The last game the Braves played in County Stadium was on Sep. 22nd, 1965 against the Los Angeles Dodgers in a 7-6 loss. The crowd that watched the Braves for one last time in Milwaukee was recorded at 12, 577. For the '65 campaign, the Braves were only able to draw 555,584 in the Lame Duck season.

19. With the nation's population shift heading to the south, Atlanta was poised to "grow up" with having a major league baseball club and eventually other professional sports in the city. With no other baseball teams close to the Braves in the Southeast, they could turn a nice profit, build a huge following, and secure t.v. and radio rights. It was a win-win for the owners, the front office, and the fans and a chance for the city of Atlanta to become the "Gateway to the South".

20. In the first game in the newly constructed Atlanta Stadium (Later to be named Fulton-County Stadium), the Braves hooked up with the Pittsburgh Pirates in a 13-inning game where the Braves lost, 3-2. The fans, all 50,671 of them, saw Tony Cloninger pitch 13 innings in his first start of the season and future New York Yankees manager Joe Torre smacked 2 home runs in the Braves' debut in the Peach State.

21. The Atlanta Braves in the 1960s had some ups and downs. The biggest upheaval since the move from Milwaukee was the Braves winning the NL West Division, something new to baseball at the time in 1969. Their playoff rivals would be the New York Mets, the "Amazin' Mets" as they were called. The Braves fell to the Mets 3 games to 0.

22. In the 1970s, Braves compiled a decade record of 725-883. The highlights of that decade were: Davey Johnson, Henry Aaron, and Darrell Evans becoming the first trio in history at that point in time to hit 40 home runs or more on the same team. Henry Aaron tied and surpassed the immortal Babe Ruth's all-time home run record on April 8th, 1974, and under the radar in the same game, Aaron scored a run, breaking Willie Mays all-time National League runs scored record at 2,063.

23. In the 1970s, Atlanta Braves also saw Hall of Famer Phil Niekro have some of the best years of his career. He led the National League in wins twice (1974-20, 1979-21) and completed games (1974-18, 1977-20, 1978-22, and 1979-23) and even lost 3 times in (1977-20, 1978-18 and 1979-20). Phil Niekro has the distinction of leading the NL in wins and loses both in the same season (1979).

24. The '80s saw future Braves stars Dale Murphy, Bob Horner, Glen Hubbard emerge as Niekro began to close out his career. The Braves in 1982 began their march to the playoffs that season by winning the first 13 games of the season and when the season was over, the Braves found themselves with another NL West Division crown, their 2nd since coming to Atlanta. But just like in 1969, they would be swept by the Cardinals 3-0. The Braves would never get back to the postseason in the '80s. Their failure as a team would give them the dubious distinction of having lost the most games than any other franchise from 1966-1990.

25. Aside from the NL West crown in 1982, Braves immortal Dale Murphy captured 2 back two back MVP awards (1982, 1983) and was the first Brave since Henry Aaron back in 1957 to win the award.

26. The 1990s saw the Braves turn a complete about-face in baseball. Going from worst to first in 1991, the Braves would roll the National League earning themselves a trip to the World Series 5 times (1991, 1992, 1995, 1996, 1999).

27. The Team of the '90s, as several sportswriters and pundits called them, turned out 6 Cy Young Winners: Glavine-(1991, 1998) Greg Maddux-(1993,1994, 1995). John Smoltz-(1996).

28. Also, the Atlanta Braves of the 1990s produced 2 MVPs in Terry Pendleton (1991) and Chipper Jones (1999). Although they were the Team of the 1990s, the Braves only walked away with 1 World Series championship (1995). And the team won a monstrous 14 division titles in a row from 1991-2005.

29. In 1982, the Braves won the Western Division on the last day of the season. The media asked team owner Ted Turner what made this club different from the losing teams of the seventies and he replied, "We have no crazies, flakes, or drug addicts.

30. Their park has a Waffle House. In July, Turner Field became the first MLB park to host a Waffle House concession stand — even if it doesn't stay open 24/7. The pairing seems fitting since both the Braves and Waffle House enjoyed immense popularity throughout the Southeastern United States. And Braves players get to enjoy pregame Waffle House.

31. Andrelton Simmons' defense. The Braves shortstop hasn't hit a ton in his first full season in the bigs, but he has established himself as one of the game's most valuable defenders with excellent range, a great arm, and good instincts in the middle infield. By defensive runs saved, he has been by far the best shortstop in the Majors in 2013.

32. The best nickname in baseball: Evan Gattis became a folk hero for his massive homers while playing in Venezuela and earned the nickname "El Oso Blanco" — Spanish for "The White Bear." He has also got one of the game's most interesting backstories. The 27-year-old rookie spent four years out of baseball after high school, working a series of odd jobs including janitor and ski-lift operator. His nametag from his days as a janitor also serves as his Twitter avatar.

33. The second-best nickname in baseball: Ever wonder why a guy named Melvin Emanuel Upton goes by the initials B.J.? It's short for Bossman Junior. Mr. Upton is the original Bossman. B.J. 's younger brother Justin is the more productive Upton in the Braves' outfield, but no one ever called him Bossman.

34. The Braves are 43-26 against their division in 2013 and have been in first place since April 7. But on top of that, the title marks their 12th since their first full season in the division in 1995. They have won 63

percent of NL East pennants since they joined the division.

35. Craig Kimbrel is incredible. Few dispute that Mariano Rivera is the best closer of all time, and Kimbrel's only in his third full season in the Majors. But the 25-year-old fireballer has a 1.34 career ERA, and his 2012 and 2013 seasons were both better than the best of Rivera's career.

36. The Braves' bullpen has the best ERA of any relief corps in the game — and that's with mainstays Johnny Venters and Eric O'Flaherty both out for the season with injuries. Luis Avilan has picked up the slack for the missing lefties, and righty David Carpenter has dominated in a setup role.

37. Freddie Freeman looks like Buzz from Home Alone. Freddie Freeman will feed you to his tarantula.

38. Colombia doesn't produce professional ballplayers at nearly the rate of its neighbor, Venezuela. Only six players born in Colombia saw big-league time in 2013, with Braves starter Julio Teheran looking like the best. Andrelton Simmons has been the most valuable of the six active Major Leaguers from Curacao in 2013, though electrifying Dodgers closer Kenley Jansen also has a case.

39. It's not really clear why Johnson pretended to be a NASCAR driver in an on-field interview in August. But it's definitely appreciated.

40. They have Dan Uggla and he's one of the most entertaining guys to watch play baseball. Uggla is 205 pounds of forearms, and he takes mighty swings. He doesn't connect as often as he used to, but he's still good for 20 homers a season.

41. They're not afraid of ghosts: Most of them aren't, at least. Chris Johnson and Tim Hudson braves Milwaukee's notorious Pfister Hotel even after B.J. Upton, Justin Upton and Jason Heyward opted to stay elsewhere.

II. ATLANTA BRAVES TEAM HISTORY

1. *The 19th century*

The longest continuing major league franchise, the Braves were founded in 1871. The Red Stockings, as they were originally named, dominated the NA with four pennants before the league broke up and the team fled to the National League for that circuit's inaugural 1876 campaign. More success followed, with eight more pennants—including four during the 1890s behind pitching rock Kid Nichols (who averaged nearly 30 wins during the decade) and a bludgeoning 1894 squad that hit .331, scored nine runs per game, and was paced by Hugh Duffy's .440 average—the highest ever recorded, modern or pre-modern.

2. The 1900s

The franchise tumbled badly into the new century, stung by the birth of the crosstown AL Red Sox and a severe lack of stability created from a merry-go-round of changing ownership. Horrible hitting made life horrible for the pitching staff; in back-to-back years (1905-06), Boston fielded four 20-game losers. Hall-of-Fame pitcher Vic Willis suffered the worst of the punishment, losing a modern-era 29 games in 1905 before escaping to a far superior Pittsburgh team.

3. The 1910s

The Braves' losing ways got worse before things got better—and when they did, it came with blindsiding force, streaking out of the last place midway through the 1914 season like a team possessed to capture the NL pennant in advance of a remarkable sweep of the heavily-favored Philadelphia Athletics in the World Series. The spoils of the "Miracle Braves" championship included several years of stability and a new home (the 43,000-seat Braves Field, at the time the majors' largest ballpark), but futility returned by decade's end.

It appeared to be business as usual for the Boston Braves. They had just reclaimed the National League basement after being swept in a doubleheader against Brooklyn, running their losing streak to five.

Adding insult to incompetence, they then traveled to Buffalo to play an exhibition against the town's minor league team—and lost, 10-2.

With a 26-40 record in early July, the Braves were doing what they had been doing for 10 years: Looking up in the standings. Way up.

But from that abysmal day in Buffalo lay the foundation for one of baseball's unlikeliest and greatest rises from oblivion. And when the season concluded in October, the rampaging Braves would completely lay waste to everyone within their path— including the three-time defending NL champion Giants, and the high-powered Philadelphia Athletics in a stunning World Series sweep.

For a decade, Boston had been the NL's perennial derelict. It certainly wasn't for a lack of instability. Over this period, the team averaged nearly 100 losses a year under seven different managers, four different owners, and under four different nicknames. While other teams stayed competitive and moved into steel-and-concrete palaces, the Braves played their dreadful brand of ball in a rickety wooden ballpark with 10,000 seats—most of them rarely occupied.

Before 1912, the franchise was purchased by former star pitcher John Montgomery Ward and two former high-ranking New York policemen, James Gaffney and John Carroll. Under their leadership, the team didn't make any immediate inroads on the field. But at least they gave the team a name that would stick: The Braves.

In 1913, the Braves named their manager George Stallings, who like Connie Mack wore suits in the dugout, but like John McGraw had a vicious temper—even worse, many claimed. Stallings prodded the Braves to a 69-82 record, which by the numbers was his worst managerial performance over the past 10 years. But it was a godsend to the Braves' faithful; it was Boston's best finish since 1902.

For 1914, Stallings chucked away veteran players he felt had stuck around too long, injected more youth into the starting lineup, and made one newsworthy acquisition. Johnny Evers wanted no part of being with the Chicago Cubs any longer and threatened to jump to the Federal League; instead, he signed with the Braves for a nice salary. The long-time second baseman was not a superstar slugger who could carry a team offensively, but his experience playing for and managing a consistently successful unit like the Cubs would engender him into a critical leadership role in Boston.

4. **The 1920s**

The Braves played the role of lambs during the Roaring' Twenties, falling behind the times by maintaining a dead-ball era attitude while the rest of baseball powered up. Only once during the decade did the Braves manage a winning season (in 1921, at 79-74) but otherwise lost a yearly average of 95 games—ironically bottoming out in 1928 despite the presence of star hitter Rogers Hornsby, who managed to escape after one year. Judge Emil Fuchs, who bought the Braves in 1923, showed his displeasure for the lack of progress by naming himself manager in 1929 (he lost 98 games).

5. **The 1930s**

Respectability returned to the franchise early in the 1930s thanks to esteemed manager Bill McKechnie and power hitter Wally Berger, who almost single-handedly shouldered the Braves' offense for six years. But it all fell apart in 1935 when Fuchs brought in an aging Babe Ruth with the (empty) promise of front office involvement, resulting in a 38-115 record that's the worst in modern NL history. In an attempt to shed the losing image, the Braves were renamed the Bees in 1936; the rebrand lasted only five years.

6. **The 1940s**

   The Braves struggled through the war years, failing to shake their standing as second division nomads despite the star exploits of outfielder Tommy Holmes. But worldwide peace brought new hope for the team, and the emergence of Warren Spahn and Johnny Sain—A-list pitchers the Braves had badly lacked for 30 years—gradually helped lift the team to contender status, peaking in 1948 with its first NL pennant in 34 years before losing a six-game World Series to Cleveland.

7. **The 1950s**

   An early-decade decline in play led to a stunning collapse at the gate, forcing owner Lou Perini to okay the majors' first relocation in 50 years when he shifted the Braves to Milwaukee. The move's impact was instant and historic; the Braves shattered NL attendance records in Wisconsin, and the team responded with two NL pennants and a world championship in 1957 behind future Hall-of-Famers Hank Aaron, Eddie Mathews, and Spahn, who averaged 20 wins per year during the 1950s.

8. **The 1960s**

   The honeymoon had barely ended in Milwaukee when the divorce took place. A combination of fan complacency and dissatisfaction with ownership led to an unexpected second move by the Braves in 13 years; Atlanta would be the next stop. Constant success became more fleeting but the Braves remained entertaining on the field, with Aaron continuing to dominate. Atlanta's first postseason appearance took place in 1969 but the Braves fell short in the inaugural NLCS to that "other" miracle team, the New York Mets.

9. **The 1970s**

The Braves entered a substandard period that was offset, early in the decade, by Aaron's high-profile chase of Babe Ruth's all-time home run record; exhausted and often mentally tortured by the limelight and bigoted hate mail, Aaron finally surpassed Ruth with his 715th career homer in 1974. A hangover ensued for the franchise and attendance began to sag; the late 1970s were notable only for the colorful (and often annoying, to other owners) shenanigans of new Atlanta lord Ted Turner and the knuckleballer antics of tireless pitcher Phil Niekro.

10. **The 1980s**

The Braves finally found solid footing in 1982 when they were sparked by squeaky-clean slugger Dale Murphy and a solid supporting cast to earn their first postseason appearance in 13 years. The resurgence re-awoke Atlanta fans and the Braves enjoyed a national following through Turner's nationwide cable outlet WTBS, self-proclaiming themselves as "America's Team." But reality set back in during the late 1980s as the Braves badly regressed in the standings—and at the gate.

11. *The 1990s*

After another last-place finish to start the decade, the Braves stunned the nation with an unprecedented worst-to-first campaign, riding excellent pitching from John Smoltz and Tom Glavine and spirited leadership from third baseman Terry Pendleton to the World Series—where they lost a memorable seven-game set to Minnesota. Hooking in future Hall-of-Famers in ace pitcher Greg Maddux and infielder Chipper Jones only heightened the Braves' decade of dominance—finishing first in their division every year throughout the 1990s except the strike-shortened 1994 season. The postseason play proved much less successful, as the Braves snagged only one World Series title, in 1995.

12. *The 2000s*

The Braves maintained their excellence through 2005 behind the veteran and crusty manager Bobby Cox, but success continued to elude them in the postseason, failing even to win one NL pennant. After placing first for 14 of 15 seasons, the Braves finally slid toward commonality, showing signs of a rebirth at the decade's end with a refreshed rotation led by Tim

Hudson and Jair Jurrjens. Through it all, Chipper Jones remained the team leader, playing at an All-Star level well into his 30s to help keep the Braves respectable.

13. **The 2010s**

Cox presided over one final season to start and returned to the postseason—and after his departure, successor Fredi Gonzalez kept the winning spirit going with the arrival of tough-as-nails first baseman Freddie Freeman and a stingy bullpen led by top closer Craig Kimbrel. A mid-decade downturn led to a housecleaning—and then a move to a new house, as the Braves departed Turner Field after just 20 years for Truist Park in Cobb County, closer to the majority of their fan base. The Braves experienced a fast-track rebound in decades thanks to exciting new blood in speedy Ronald Acuna Jr. and second baseman Ozzie Albies.

III. GREATEST BRAVES PLAYERS OF ALL -TIME

A. *Henry Aaron*

1. Name Note: commonly referred to as Hank Aaron

2. Positions: Rightfielder and First Baseman

3. Bats: Right • Throws: Right

4. 6-0, 180lb (183cm, 81kg)

5. Born: February 5, 1934, in Mobile, AL

6. Died: January 22, 2021 (Aged 86-352d) in Atlanta, GA

7. Buried: Southview Cemetery, Atlanta, GA

8. High School: Allen Institute (Mobile, AL)

9. Debut: April 13, 1954 (Age 20-067d, 11,084th in major league history) vs. CIN 5 AB, 0 H, 0 HR, 0 RBI, 0 SB

10. Last Game: October 3, 1976 (Age 42-241d) vs. DET 3 AB, 1 H, 0 HR, 1 RBI, 0 SB

11. Hall of Fame: Inducted as Player in 1982. (Voted by BBWAA on 406/415 ballots)

12. Rookie Status: Exceeded rookie limits during 1954 season

13. Full Name: Henry Louis Aaron

14. Nicknames: Hammer, Hammerin' Hank, or Bad Henry

B. *Kid Nichols*

1. Position: Pitcher

2. Bats: Both • Throws: Right

3. 5-10, 175lb (178cm, 79kg)

4. Born: September 14, 1869 in Madison, WI

5. Died: April 11, 1953 (Aged 83-209d) in Kansas City, MO

6. Buried: Mount Moriah Cemetery, Kansas City, MO

7. Debut: April 23, 1890 (Age 20-221d, 1,453rd in major league history)

8. Last Game: May 18, 1906 (Age 36-246d) vs. CHC 0.1 IP, 2 H, 0 SO, 2 BB, 0 ER

9. Hall of Fame: Inducted as Player in 1949. (Voted by Old Timers Committee)

10. Rookie Status: Exceeded rookie limits during 1890 season

11. Full Name: Charles Augustus Nichols

C. *Warren Spahn*

1. Position: Pitcher

2. Bats: Left • Throws: Left

3. 6-0, 172lb (183cm, 78kg)

4. Born: April 23, 1921 in Buffalo, NY

5. Died: November 24, 2003 (Aged 82-215d) in Broken Arrow, OK

6. Buried: Elmwood Cemetery, Hartshorne, OK

7. High School: South Park HS (Buffalo, NY)

8. Debut: April 19, 1942 (Age 20-361d, 9,246th in major league history) vs. NYG 0.2 IP, 0 H, 0 SO, 0 BB, 0 ER

9. Last Game: October 1, 1965 (Age 44-161d) vs. CIN 0.1 IP, 1 H, 0 SO, 1 BB, 0 ER

10. Hall of Fame: Inducted as Player in 1973. (Voted by BBWAA on 316/380 ballots)

11. Rookie Status: Exceeded rookie limits during 1946 season

12. Full Name: Warren Edward Spahn

D. *Eddie Mathews*

1. Positions: Third Baseman and First Baseman

2. Bats: Left • Throws: Right

3. 6-1, 190lb (185cm, 86kg)

4. Born: October 13, 1931 in Texarkana, TX

5. Died: February 18, 2001 (Aged 69-128d) in La Jolla, CA

6. Buried: Santa Barbara Cemetery, Santa Barbara, CA

7. High School: Santa Barbara HS (Santa Barbara, CA)

8. Debut: April 15, 1952 (Age 20-185d, 10,883rd in major league history) vs. BRO 3 AB, 0 H, 0 HR, 0 RBI, 0 SB

9. Last Game: September 27, 1968 (Age 36-350d) vs. WSA 1 AB, 0 H, 0 HR, 0 RBI, 0 SB

10. Hall of Fame: Inducted as Player in 1978. (Voted by BBWAA on 301/379 ballots)

11. Rookie Status: Exceeded rookie limits during 1952 season

12. Full Name: Edwin Lee Mathews

13. Nicknames: Eddie Mattress, Cap'n Eddie, Santa Barbara Bomber or Brookfield Bomber

E. *Phil Niekro*

1. Position: Pitcher

2. Bats: Right • Throws: Right

3. 6-1, 180lb (185cm, 81kg)

4. Born: April 1, 1939 in Blaine, OH

5. Died: December 27, 2020 (Aged 81-270d) in Flowery Branch, GA

6. Buried: Memorial Park South Cemetery, Flowery Branch, GA

7. High School: Bridgeport HS (Bridgeport, OH)

8. Debut: April 15, 1964 (Age 25-014d, 12,217th in major league history) vs. SFG 0.1 IP, 0 H, 0 SO, 0 BB, 0 ER

9. Last Game: September 27, 1987 (Age 48-179d) vs. SFG 3.0 IP, 6 H, 0 SO, 6 BB, 5 ER

10. Hall of Fame: Inducted as Player in 1997. (Voted by BBWAA on 380/473 ballots)

11. Rookie Status: Exceeded rookie limits during 1965 season

12. Agents: Bruce Church

13. Full Name: Philip Henry Niekro

14. Nicknames: Knucksie

15. Pronunciation: \NEE-kro\

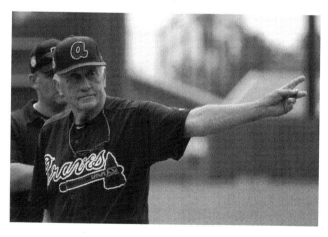

F. Chipper Jones

1. Positions: Third Baseman and Leftfielder

2. Bats: Both • Throws: Right

3. 6-4, 210lb (193cm, 95kg)

4. Born: April 24, 1972 (Age: 49-060d) in DeLand, FL

5. Draft: Drafted by the Atlanta Braves in the 1st round (1st) of the 1990 MLB June Amateur Draft from The Bolles School (Jacksonville, FL).

6. High School: The Bolles School (Jacksonville, FL)

7. Debut: September 11, 1993 (Age 21-140d, 16,444th in major league history) vs. SDP 0 AB, 0 H, 0 HR, 0 RBI, 0 SB

8. Last Game: October 3, 2012 (Age 40-162d) vs. PIT 1 AB, 1 H, 0 HR, 0 RBI, 0 SB

9. Hall of Fame: Inducted as Player in 2018. (Voted by BBWAA on 410/422 ballots)

10. Rookie Status: Exceeded rookie limits during 1995 season

11. Agents: Jet Sports Management (B.B. Abbott)

12. National Team: USA (WBC)

13. Full Name: Larry Wayne Jones

G. *John Smoltz*

1. Position: Pitcher

2. Bats: Right • Throws: Right

3. 6-3, 210lb (190cm, 95kg)

4. Born: May 15, 1967 (Age: 54-039d) in Detroit, MI

5. Draft: Drafted by the Detroit Tigers in the 22nd round of the 1985 MLB June Amateur Draft from Waverly HS (Lansing, MI).

6. High School: Waverly HS (Lansing, MI)

7. Debut: July 23, 1988 (Age 21-069d, 15,517th in major league history) vs. NYM 8.0 IP, 4 H, 2 SO, 1 BB, 1 ER, W

8. Last Game: September 30, 2009 (Age 42-138d) vs. CIN 4.0 IP, 6 H, 3 SO, 5 BB, 6 ER, L

9. Hall of Fame: Inducted as Player in 2015. (Voted by BBWAA on 455/549 ballots)

10. Rookie Status: Exceeded rookie limits during 1988 season

11. Agents: Lonnie Cooper, Myles Shoda

12. National Team: USA (18U)

13. Full Name: John Andrew Smoltz

14. Nicknames: Smoltzie

H. *Greg Maddux*

1. Position: Pitcher

2. Bats: Right • Throws: Right

3. 6-0, 170lb (183cm, 77kg)

4. Born: April 14, 1966 (Age: 55-070d) in San Angelo, TX

5. Draft: Drafted by the Chicago Cubs in the 2nd round of the 1984 MLB June Amateur Draft from Valley HS (Las Vegas, NV).

6. High School: Valley HS (Las Vegas, NV)

7. Debut: September 2, 1986 (Age 20-141d, 15,238th in major league history) vs. HOU 1.0 IP, 1 H, 1 SO, 0 BB, 1 ER, L *

   (*game was a suspended game and the player actually debuted the day following the day listed.)

8. Last Game: September 27, 2008 (Age 42-166d) vs. SFG 6.0 IP, 2 H, 2 SO, 0 BB, 1 ER, W

9. Hall of Fame: Inducted as Player in 2014. (Voted by BBWAA on 555/571 ballots)

10. Rookie Status: Exceeded rookie limits during 1987 season

11. Agents: Scott Boras

12. Full Name: Gregory Alan Maddux

13. Nicknames: Mad Dog or The Professor

14. Pronunciation: \MADD-ucks\

I. **Tom Glavine**

1. Position: Pitcher

2. Bats: Left • Throws: Left

3. 6-0, 175lb (183cm, 79kg)

4. Born: March 25, 1966 (Age: 55-090d) in Concord, MA

5. Draft: Drafted by the Atlanta Braves in the 2nd round of the 1984 MLB June Amateur Draft from Billerica HS (Billerica, MA).

6. High School: Billerica HS (Billerica, MA)

7. Debut: August 17, 1987 (Age 21-145d, 15,388th in major league history) vs. HOU 3.2 IP, 10 H, 1 SO, 5 BB, 6 ER, L

8. Last Game: August 14, 2008 (Age 42-142d) vs. CHC 4.0 IP, 7 H, 3 SO, 4 BB, 7 ER, L

9. Hall of Fame: Inducted as Player in 2014. (Voted by BBWAA on 525/571 ballots)

10. Rookie Status: Exceeded rookie limits during 1987 season

11. Agents: Gregg Clifton • Previously: Gregg Clifton

12. Full Name: Thomas Michael Glavine

13. Pronunciation: \GLA-vin\

J. *Andruw Jones*

1. Position: Centerfielder

2. Bats: Right • Throws: Right

3. 6-1, 225lb (185cm, 102kg)

4. Born: April 23, 1977 (Age: 44-061d) in Willemstad, Curacao

5. High School: St. Paulus (Willemstad, Curacao)

6. Debut: August 15, 1996 (Age 19-114d, 16,959th in major league history) vs. PHI 5 AB, 1 H, 0 HR, 1 RBI, 0 SB

7. Last Game: October 3, 2012 (Age 35-163d) vs. BOS 1 AB, 0 H, 0 HR, 0 RBI, 0 SB

8. Rookie Status: Exceeded rookie limits during 1997 season

9. Agents: Scott Boras

10. Full Name: Andruw Rudolf Jones

11. Nicknames: The Curaçao Kid

12. Pronunciation: \Andrew\

K. Dale Murphy

1. Positions: Outfielder, First Baseman and Catcher

2. Bats: Right • Throws: Right

3. 6-4, 210lb (193cm, 95kg)

4. Born: March 12, 1956 (Age: 65-103d) in Portland, OR

5. Draft: Drafted by the Atlanta Braves in the 1st round (5th) of the 1974 MLB June Amateur Draft from Woodrow Wilson HS (Portland, OR).

6. High School: Woodrow Wilson HS (Portland, OR)

7. School: Brigham Young University (Provo, UT)

8. Debut: September 13, 1976 (Age 20-185d, 13,827th in major league history) vs. LAD 4 AB, 2 H, 0 HR, 2 RBI, 0 SB

9. Last Game: May 21, 1993 (Age 37-070d) vs. LAD 3 AB, 0 H, 0 HR, 0 RBI, 0 SB

10. Rookie Status: Exceeded rookie limits during 1977 season

11. Agents: Bruce Church

12. Full Name: Dale Bryan Murphy

13. Nicknames: The Murph

L. Bob Gibson

1. Position: Pitcher

2. Bats: Right • Throws: Right

3. 6-1, 189lb (185cm, 85kg)

4. Born: November 9, 1935 in Omaha, NE

5. Died: October 2, 2020 (Aged 84-328d) in Omaha, NE

6. High School: Tech HS (Omaha, NE)

7. School: Creighton University (Omaha, NE)

8. Debut: April 15, 1959 (Age 23-157d, 11,634th in major league history) vs. LAD 2.0 IP, 2 H, 0 SO, 0 BB, 2 ER

9. Last Game: September 3, 1975 (Age 39-298d) vs. CHC 1.0 IP, 2 H, 0 SO, 3 BB, 5 ER, L

10. Hall of Fame: Inducted as Player in 1981. (Voted by BBWAA on 337/401 ballots)

11. Rookie Status: Exceeded rookie limits during 1959 season

12. Full Name: Robert Gibson

13. Nicknames: Hoot or Gibby

M. Barry Bonds

1. Position: Leftfielder

2. Bats: Left • Throws: Left

3. 6-1, 185lb (185cm, 83kg)

4. Born: July 24, 1964 (Age: 56-335d) in Riverside, CA us

5. Draft: Drafted by the San Francisco Giants in the 2nd round of the 1982 MLB June Amateur Draft from Junipero Serra HS (San Mateo, CA) and the Pittsburgh Pirates in the 1st round (6th) of the 1985 MLB June Amateur Draft from Arizona State University (Tempe, AZ).

6. High School: Junipero Serra HS (San Mateo, CA)

7. School: Arizona State University (Tempe, AZ)

8. Debut: May 30, 1986 (Age 21-310d, 15,179th in major league history) vs. LAD 5 AB, 0 H, 0 HR, 0 RBI, 0 SB

9. Last Game: September 26, 2007 (Age 43-064d) vs. SDP 3 AB, 0 H, 0 HR, 0 RBI, 0 SB

10. Rookie Status: Exceeded rookie limits during 1986 season

11. Agents: Jeff Borris • Previously: Dennis Gilbert, Rod Wright, Scott Boras

12. Full Name: Barry Lamar Bonds

Quiz Answers

1. B	25. A	49. C
2. B	26. B	50. A
3. D	27. C	51. C
4. C	28. A	52. C
5. D	29. C	53. A
6. A	30. D	54. A
7. B	31. D	55. D
8. D	32. B	56. B
9. A	33. A	57. C
10. A	34. D	58. D
11. A	35. C	59. C
12. B	36. A	60. C
13. D	37. A	61. C
14. C	38. C	62. A
15. B	39. A	63. D
16. D	40. A	64. C
17. A	41. D	65. B
18. D	42. B	66. A
19. A	43. D	67. C
20. B	44. D	68. C
21. B	45. C	69. C
22. C	46. A	70. A
23. D	47. C	71. A
24. A	48. A	72. B

73. D	89. B	105. C
74. D	90. B	106. C
75. C	91. D	107. A
76. C	92. C	108. B
77. D	93. C	109. D
78. A	94. B	110. B
79. D	95. B	111. D
80. C	96. B	112. D
81. C	97. C	113. B
82. D	98. B	114. C
83. A	99. A	115. D
84. A	100. C	116. A
85. D	101. D	117. D
86. A	102. A	118. B
87. C	103. D	119. D
88. D	104. B	120. B

Thank You For Reading!

Is there anything you would like to add?

_____

_____

_____

_____

_____

_____

_____

_____

_____

_____

_____

_____

_____

_____

Who is your favorite Braves' player? Why?

_____

_____

_____

_____

_____

_____

_____

_____

_____

_____

_____

_____

_____

_____

Stick your memorable photos with the Atlanta Braves games here!

Made in the USA
Columbia, SC
08 November 2021